CECIL COUNTY PUBLIC LIBRARY
ELKTON, MARYLAND 21921

D1305548

PRESIDENTS

President John F. Kennedy and John F. Kennedy, Jr.

PRESIDENTS

A LIBRARY OF CONGRESS BOOK

BY MARTIN W. SANDLER

Introduction by James H. Billington, Librarian of Congress

HarperCollins*Publishers*

For Rachel and Alex Schlow, two special young friends

ACKNOWLEDGMENTS

The author wishes to thank Robert Dierker, former senior advisor for multimedia activities of the Library of Congress, and Dana Pratt, former director of publishing of the Library of Congress, for their important contributions to this book. Appreciation is expressed to Kate Murphy, Carol Weiss, Heather Henson, Liza Baker, Alan Bisbort, the staff of the Prints and Photographs Division of the Library of Congress and Dennis Magnu of the Library's Photoduplication Service. The author is indebted to the Jimmy Carter Library, the Gerald R. Ford Library, the Lyndon B. Johnson Library, the John F. Kennedy Library, the Richard M. Nixon Library, the Ronald Reagan Library, the Franklin D. Roosevelt Library, Wide World Photos and the White House, all of which graciously provided photographs for this book. A very special acknowledgment is made to Kate Morgan Jackson, editor par excellence.

◆

Presidents
A Library of Congress Book
Copyright © 1995 by Eagle Productions, Inc.

All rights reserved. No part of this book may be used or reproduced in any manner whatsoever without written permission except in the case of brief quotations embodied in critical articles and reviews. Printed in Mexico.
For information address HarperCollins Children's Books, a division of HarperCollins Publishers, 10 East 53rd Street, New York, NY 10022.

Library of Congress Cataloging-in-Publication Data
Sandler, Martin W.
Presidents / by Martin W. Sandler ; introduction by James H. Billington.
p.   cm.
"A Library of Congress book."
ISBN 0-06-024534-4. — ISBN 0-06-024535-2 (lib. bdg.)
1. Presidents—United States—Miscellanea.   I. Title.

E176.1.S23   1995
973—dc20

93-49403
CIP
AC

Design by Tom Starace with Jennifer Goldman
1   2   3   4   5   6   7   8   9   10
❖
First Edition

CECIL COUNTY PUBLIC LIBRARY
ELKTON, MARYLAND 21921

SEP 1 9 1995

Our type of democracy has depended upon and grown with knowledge gained through books and all the other various records of human memory and imagination. By their very nature, these records foster freedom and dignity. Historically they have been the companions of a responsible, democratic citizenry. They provide keys to the dynamism of our past and perhaps to our national competitiveness in the future. They link the record of yesterday with the possibilities of tomorrow.

One of our main purposes at the Library of Congress is to make the riches of the Library even more available to even wider circles of our multiethnic society. Thus we are proud to lend our name and resources to this series of children's books. We share Martin W. Sandler's goal of enriching our greatest natural resource—the minds and imaginations of our young people.

The scope and variety of Library of Congress print and visual materials contained in these books demonstrate that libraries are the starting places for the adventure of learning that can go on whatever one's vocation and location in life. They demonstrate that reading is an adventure like the one that is discovery itself. Being an American is not a patent of privilege but an invitation to adventure. We must go on discovering America.

James H. Billington
The Librarian of Congress

As Americans, we have long been fascinated with our presidents. In a nation where there is no royal family, president- and first family–watching has become a national pastime. Much of this is due to the power of the office, but even more is due to the fact that, above all else, the presidency is a profoundly human institution. We have learned that such things as the way a president relates to his family, the roles he carries out, the way that a president spends his leisure time and the manner in which he relates to the public all affect the way he carries out his duties and the future of the office itself.

In this book you will learn much about our presidents and their families. Along with viewing presidents at work and at play, you will meet the wives of our presidents. You will see how, in modern times, recognition of their abilities and important achievements on behalf of the nation has helped pave the way for the eventual election of our first female president. You will also meet presidential children and first family pets. You will see how all contribute in one way or another to making the presidency, as one historian has written, "one of the few truly successful institutions created by men [and women] in their endless quest for the blessings of free government."

MARTIN W. SANDLER

President Gerald Ford and family (facing page)

THE OFFICE OF THE PRESIDENT

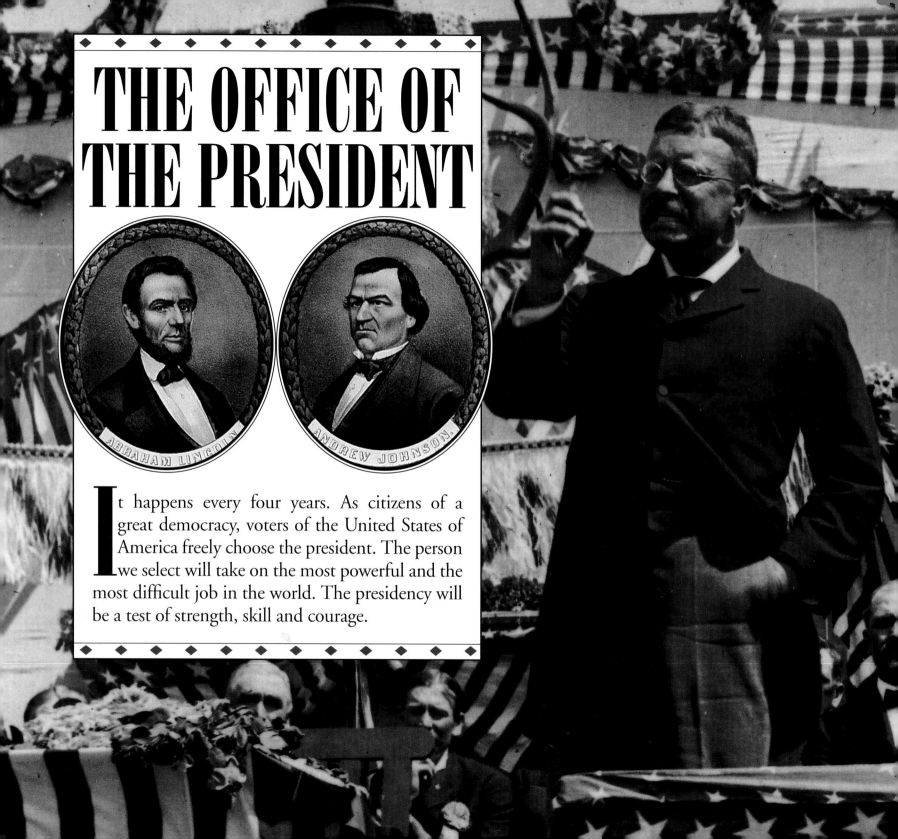

It happens every four years. As citizens of a great democracy, voters of the United States of America freely choose the president. The person we select will take on the most powerful and the most difficult job in the world. The presidency will be a test of strength, skill and courage.

General William Henry Harrison

S ince our first president was elected in 1789, hundreds of people have sought the office. They have come from many different professions. Our presidents have been lawyers, farmers, military figures, teachers, shopkeepers and full-time politicians. One was even a movie star.

Some, through their deeds and the challenges they faced, will always be remembered.

President George Washington

President Chester A. Arthur

Others have served and then passed, almost forgotten, into history.

President John F. Kennedy and family

In a nation where there is no royalty, president- and presidential family–watching has long been a national pastime. It is more than just curiosity; for along with the many roles he plays and the decisions he makes, how a president lives, how he plays, how he relates to his fellow Americans and the type of support he receives from his family set a tone for the nation and affect the mark he leaves on the presidency.

ONE OFFICE, MANY DIFFERENT PEOPLE

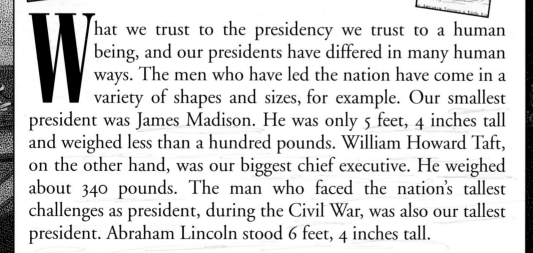

What we trust to the presidency we trust to a human being, and our presidents have differed in many human ways. The men who have led the nation have come in a variety of shapes and sizes, for example. Our smallest president was James Madison. He was only 5 feet, 4 inches tall and weighed less than a hundred pounds. William Howard Taft, on the other hand, was our biggest chief executive. He weighed about 340 pounds. The man who faced the nation's tallest challenges as president, during the Civil War, was also our tallest president. Abraham Lincoln stood 6 feet, 4 inches tall.

Our youngest elected chief executive was John F. Kennedy, who was 43 years and 236 days old when he won the presidency. Theodore Roosevelt was actually just short of 43 years old when he became president but as vice president he came to the office when President William McKinley was assassinated.

John F. Kennedy could read and understand 2,000 words a minute. Andrew Johnson was illiterate when, at age eighteen, he married Eliza McCardle. His sixteen-year-old bride taught the future president how to read and write.

Our oldest president was Ronald Reagan. The former governor of California was just sixteen days short of his seventieth birthday when he began his eight years in the White House.

Our longest-serving president was Franklin Delano Roosevelt. Before the Constitution limited a president's time in office, he served almost four full terms, from 1933 to 1945.

William Henry Harrison

Since 1951, the Constitution has limited the president's length of time in office to no more than two full four-year terms. Many of our presidents have served for eight years. Others have been in office for a single four-year term. Eight presidents either died or were assassinated during their presidency. The shortest presidency was that of William Henry Harrison, who died in office in April 1841, only one month after being inaugurated.

The longest presidential inaugural speech was delivered by the person who served the shortest period of time. William Henry Harrison's inaugural address contained 8,443 words. The shortest inaugural speech was delivered by George Washington. His second inaugural address was only 133 words long.

Herbert Hoover, who had the misfortune of being president during America's Great Depression, lived long enough after leaving office to earn a proud reputation by taking on a variety of humanitarian tasks around the world. Among the many awards he received were honorary degrees from over fifty American universities. Hoover lived for thirty-one years after leaving the White House, making him our longest-lived ex-president.

James K. Polk was one of our hardest-working presidents. During his single four-year term in office, he worked every day from sunup to well after sundown. While he was president, the United States acquired the territory that would become California, New Mexico, Arizona, Nevada, Utah and Wyoming. In addition, the Oregon boundary was established, and Texas, Iowa and Wisconsin were admitted as states. Worn out from overwork, Polk died only three months after leaving office. He was an ex-president for the shortest time of any of our presidents.

PRESIDENTIAL FIRSTS

A ll of our presidents have left their marks, and many have established "firsts" while in office. Presidential firsts are important because they reflect the history both of the presidency and of the nation itself. Martin Van Buren, for example, was the first president born as an American citizen, not a British subject. The first president to ride in a steamship was James Monroe, while Andrew Jackson was the first to ride in a train. The first president born west of the Mississippi was Herbert Hoover. John F. Kennedy was the first born in the twentieth century. The first president to appoint an African American to the Supreme Court was Lyndon B. Johnson, who selected Thurgood Marshall, a distinguished lawyer and civil rights champion.

braham Lincoln was involved in several firsts. He was the first president born outside of the original thirteen states. In 1861, he became the first president to receive a transcontinental telegram. Tragically, he was also the first president to be assassinated. On April 14, 1865, while attending a play with his wife, Lincoln was shot and mortally wounded by John Wilkes Booth, a well-known actor and a supporter of the Confederacy.

Four presidents of the United States have been assassinated while in office—Lincoln, Garfield, McKinley and Kennedy. The first attempt on a president's life was against Andrew Jackson in 1835. Assassination attempts were also made against Presidents Truman, Ford and Reagan.

Theodore (Teddy) Roosevelt was perhaps the nation's most active president. No matter when he served, he undoubtedly would have established more than his share of presidential firsts simply because of his boundless energy. As it happened, Roosevelt was president during a period of great inventiveness and change in the United States. Along with being the first president to win a Nobel Peace Prize and the first to go underwater in a submarine, Roosevelt was the first president to ride in an automobile.

He was also the first president or ex-president to fly in an airplane.

Teddy Roosevelt was also the first president to leave the United States during his term of office. In 1906, he traveled to Panama to inspect the progress being made in the building of the Panama Canal. Those who went with him knew that it would not be long before this president made his inspection a most active experience.

The first African American candidate for president or vice president was Frederick Douglass, who was nominated for the vice presidency by the People's party in 1872. The first African American to run for the presidency was Clennon King, the candidate of the Independent Afro-American party in 1960. The first woman presidential candidate was Victoria Claflin Woodhull, who was nominated in 1872 by the Equal Rights party.

Like Theodore Roosevelt, other presidents owe many of the firsts they established to the technological achievements of the time when they served. In 1921, Warren Harding became the first president to ride to his inauguration in an automobile. One year later, he became the first president to broadcast a speech over the radio.

Many presidential firsts are associated with what have become established American traditions. William Howard Taft was the first president to officially open the major-league baseball season by throwing out the first ball.

Calvin Coolidge, who succeeded Harding, was the first president to appear in a motion picture newsreel. Known as Silent Cal, Coolidge was famous for being a man of few words, yet the fact that he never seemed reluctant to dress in outlandish costumes for the camera made him a photographer's delight.

Before 1850, all White House cooking was done over open fireplaces. The first president to have a stove was Millard Fillmore, but neither he, his wife nor the White House cook knew how to use it. Fillmore also bathed in the first White House bathtub with running water. Electric lights were installed in the White House in 1890, but both President Benjamin Harrison and his wife, Caroline, were afraid they would get an electric shock if they turned them on.

Twenty-four years after Theodore Roosevelt left office, his cousin Franklin Delano Roosevelt became president of the United States. His twelve years in office included such momentous events as the Great Depression and World War II and enabled FDR, as he was often called, to establish more presidential firsts than any other chief executive except George Washington, who, as our first president, established firsts in almost everything he did. Franklin Roosevelt was the first president to appear on television. When he selected Frances Perkins to be secretary of labor, he became the first president to name a woman to his cabinet. As the nation's commander in chief during World War II, he traveled the globe and became the first president to leave the United States during wartime.

In modern times, advanced means of travel and fast-moving world events have made globe-hopping a presidential way of life. In the 1970's, Richard Nixon became the first president to visit all fifty states. He was also the first president to visit China while in office.

ONE-OF-A-KIND PRESIDENTS

While there have been many firsts in the presidential experience, there have also been many unique occurrences. Only once, for example, have a father and son both been presidents. They were John Adams and John Quincy Adams. Only once has a grandfather and later his grandson served in the nation's highest office. They were William Henry Harrison and Benjamin Harrison. When John Tyler's term as president was over, he got himself elected to the Confederate House of Representatives, making him our only president to serve in two governments. George Washington has a particular distinction: He was the only president who was not inaugurated in the city that would be named in his honor. When Washington took office in 1789, the city of Washington was not yet built, and our first president took his oath of office in New York City, then the capital of the United States.

There have been other unusual presidential inaugurations. When John F. Kennedy was tragically gunned down in Dallas, Texas, Vice President Lyndon B. Johnson became the only president sworn in on an airplane and the only president to be sworn in by a woman, when he was administered the oath of office on Air Force One by Judge Sarah Hughes. Calvin Coolidge is our only president to have been sworn in by his father. Upon the sudden death of Warren Harding, Coolidge's father, John, a notary public, administered the oath of office to his son at 2:00 A.M. in the Coolidge family farmhouse in Vermont.

The United States had a vice president before it had a president. Vice President John Adams was sworn in on April 21, 1789, nine days before George Washington took his oath as president.

Grover Cleveland was the only president to be married in the White House. His bride's father had been Cleveland's law partner, and Cleveland had known his future wife from the day she was born. He had, in fact, bought her her first baby carriage.

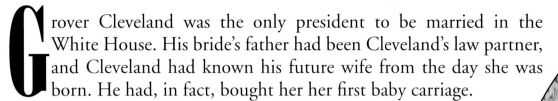

Grover Cleveland served as president from 1885 to 1889. When he ran for a second term, he was defeated by Benjamin Harrison. In 1892, however, Cleveland ran again and won back the presidency. He is our only president to have served two nonconsecutive terms.

James Buchanan was the only one of our presidents who was never married.

Thomas Jefferson's varied and extraordinary accomplishments made him the most gifted president the nation has ever known. He wrote the Declaration of Independence and was a framer of our Constitution. He was the first governor of a state to be elected president and the first president who had served as secretary of state. He was an accomplished inventor, architect, scientist and musician. He was our only president to have designed his own home and to have founded a major university, the University of Virginia. After he died, his library became the beginning of the nation's Library of Congress. The epitaph he wrote to be placed on his tombstone over his grave did not even mention all he had accomplished as president. It stated, "Here was buried Thomas Jefferson, author of the Declaration of American Independence, of the Statute of Virginia for religious freedom, and father of the University of Virginia."

Thomas Jefferson never applied for a patent for any of his inventions. The only president to have a patent issued in his name was Abraham Lincoln, who invented a hydraulic device that could lift ships over shoals.

Andrew Jackson became a military hero at the Battle of New Orleans during the War of 1812. Above everything else, it seemed, Andy loved a good fight. It is believed that in the years before he became president, he fought more than one hundred duels and killed several men. When he was in the White House, he had a bullet from one of these fights removed from his arm. Another bullet remained lodged near his heart for the rest of his life.

Each of our presidents has viewed his White House experience in his own way. Thomas Jefferson called it "splendid misery." Harry Truman felt that being president was like having a tiger at one's tail every hour of the day. Theodore Roosevelt, on the other hand, loved every minute of his presidency and called his office a "bully pulpit." William Howard Taft's desire was to be something other than president. More than anything else, he wanted to be chief justice of the Supreme Court. When his eight years as president were over, he got his wish—President Warren Harding appointed him to the post. As chief justice, Taft had the pleasure of swearing in both Calvin Coolidge and Herbert Hoover. Said a happy Chief Justice Taft, "In my present life I don't remember that I ever was President."

James Monroe is the only president to have a foreign capital city named after him—Monrovia in Liberia. Woodrow Wilson is the only president to have earned a Ph.D. John Kennedy is the only president to have been awarded the Pulitzer Prize—for biography. Dwight Eisenhower is the only president to have held a pilot's license.

While the majority of our presidents have been either lawyers, military men or full-time politicians, many have come from a variety of other backgrounds. Andrew Johnson was a tailor. Harry Truman owned a clothing store. Millard Fillmore was apprenticed to a cloth maker. James Garfield was first a teacher and then a college president. Jimmy Carter owned a peanut farm. One of our presidents came to the White House from an unlikely background. Before entering politics, Ronald Reagan was a movie star. Reagan appeared in more than fifty Hollywood movies and was the host for two major television series.

In 1974, as a result of mounting evidence that Richard Nixon had been personally involved in covering up a burglary by his campaign staff, impeachment proceedings were begun against him. Before the impeachment trial could begin, Nixon became our only president to resign from office.

The demands on a president are such that no chief executive can serve without making political enemies. Many presidential administrations have been marred by scandal as well. Only twice in our history has political opposition or scandal been so serious that impeachment proceedings (a trial in Congress to see if the president should be removed) were brought against a sitting president. In 1868, congressmen opposed to Andrew Johnson's post–Civil War policies impeached the president. In the impeachment trial, Johnson was found not guilty by a single vote.

CECIL COUNTY PUBLIC LIBRARY
ELKTON, MARYLAND 21921

A MAN OF THE PEOPLE

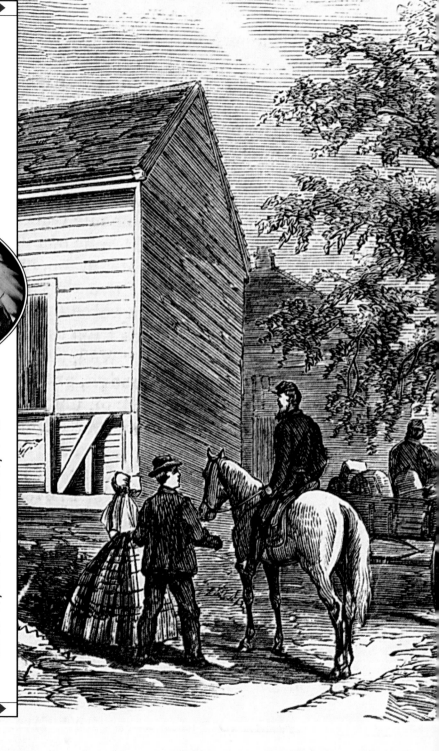

The person who occupies the White House assumes many roles. Among other responsibilities, he is our chief executive, our chief of state, the head of his political party and our commander in chief. He is also a human being, however. Over the years, most of our presidents have attempted in various ways to present themselves as men of the people. They have tried to show the public that, despite the trappings of their office, they still possess the common touch. It is a natural inclination and an accepted political strategy.

The first true "man of the people" to be elected president was Andrew Jackson. He was our first chief executive not descended from an old wealthy family. On the evening of his first inauguration, Jackson invited the public to a reception at the White House. More than 20,000 of his ardent supporters jammed the building and turned the reception into a near riot. They tracked mud through the White House, ruined rugs and furniture and caused thousands of dollars' worth of damage. Refreshments included an enormous 1,400-pound cheese, parts of which were also trampled into the furniture and rugs, causing an odor that remained in the Executive Mansion throughout the first months of the Jackson presidency.

Before winning the presidential election of 1860, Abraham Lincoln had lost eight elections for various offices.

Abraham Lincoln, like Jackson, was a man of the people, having come from humble beginnings. He was born in a log cabin and, as a young man, earned his living as a rail splitter. After he entered politics, those who ran his campaigns for office made sure that Lincoln's simple, folksy beginnings were widely portrayed.

Throughout the 1800's, people who ran political campaigns saw that it was good for the campaign to present their candidate as having come from humble beginnings, even if those candidates were born into wealth. Whether they had been born in one or not, the simple log cabin became an important political symbol for a succession of men who sought the nation's highest office.

There were other widely used political symbols, all included to portray the candidate as a man of the people. Many campaign posters featured images of "the little red schoolhouse," a nostalgic favorite of voters everywhere. Candidates were also portrayed as defenders of the American farm, although millions of citizens were increasingly moving to towns and cities.

From our early days as a nation, the eagle has been both our national bird and the most widely used of all political symbols. The country almost had a much different national symbol. Benjamin Franklin proposed the use of the more common wild turkey, but his wishes were turned down in favor of the more majestic American bald eagle.

By the end of the 1800's, the portrayal of presidents as humble men of the people became such accepted practice that certain presidents even agreed to appear in advertisements. President Rutherford B. Hayes and his wife, Lucy, were shown in magazine ads endorsing a household iron. And both President Cleveland and ex-President Benjamin Harrison agreed to be portrayed together in a national beer advertisement.

As the twentieth century began, the news media made the American public increasingly aware of national and world events. The country began to expect more decorum from its presidents. It was no longer considered necessary or even politically wise for candidates and presidents falsely to claim humble beginnings. The portrayal of a president in commercial advertisements also became regarded as beneath the dignity of the office. Still, most presidents wanted to stay in touch with ordinary citizens. In the first quarter of the 1900's, presidents from William Howard Taft to Herbert Hoover reached out to the public by opening the doors of the White House on New Year's Day, giving every man, woman and child who appeared the chance to shake hands with the president of the United States.

The practice of a president's shaking hands at a public reception originated with Thomas Jefferson at a Fourth of July celebration in 1801. George Washington and John Adams, who served before Jefferson, always bowed on such occasions.

In 1993, on the day after he was inaugurated president, Bill Clinton carried out a scaled-down version of an old presidential tradition. The chief executive and his family greeted hundreds of randomly selected members of the public at the White House.

President Warren Harding

President
Harry Truman

J ust as earlier presidents used campaign symbols such as the log cabin and the little red schoolhouse to appeal to voters, twentieth-century presidents have found that fondness for children plays well with the public. Kissing babies and holding youngsters has become a common campaign tactic.

Certainly reaching out to the people is good for a president's image. For most presidents, though, it is more than a campaign tactic. The demands of the office keep a president very isolated from the public. Many chief executives would agree with Harry Truman, who called the White House "a nice prison, but a prison nevertheless."

Franklin D. Roosevelt was probably our most superstitious president.. He traveled continually but would never leave for a trip on a Friday. Although he attended countless dinners with heads of state around the world, he would not sit at a table for thirteen guests.

PRESIDENTS AT PLAY

In their attempt to relieve the pressures of their office, all our presidents have relaxed during whatever time they could steal away from their duties. Chester A. Arthur was fond of taking sleigh rides down Pennsylvania Avenue. George Washington attended cockfights and horse races. Both John Quincy Adams and James Garfield kept billiard tables at the White House. Franklin Roosevelt was an ardent stamp collector and took at least one stamp album with him wherever he traveled. Harry Truman and Richard Nixon played piano, while Thomas Jefferson and John Tyler were accomplished violinists. Many of our presidents were either golfers, hunters or fishermen. Our early presidents, like their countrymen and -women, sought relaxation in simple pleasures. Rutherford B. Hayes, for example, was fond of attending clambakes.

Although it seems hard to believe today, there was a time when our presidents felt safe traveling without a host of Secret Service agents or policemen to protect them. Even for a president, simple pleasures could be pursued in a simple way. The man standing in the center of the trolley car is President William McKinley, captured by the camera as he enjoyed a day's relaxation at one of the nation's most popular sightseeing spots, Niagara Falls.

President John Quincy Adams pursued his own special simple pleasure. Every day, weather permitting, he would get up, walk down to Washington's Potomac River, hang his clothes on a tree and swim naked in the river.

President Chester A. Arthur

Fishing has always been a popular presidential pastime, and the list of our chief executives who loved the sport includes Washington, Jefferson, Cleveland, Coolidge, Hoover, Franklin Roosevelt, Truman, Eisenhower, Lyndon Johnson, Carter and Bush. The most expert of all our presidents in this activity was probably Chester A. Arthur, who was regarded as one of the finest fishermen in all of America. His greatest catch was an eighty-pound bass, which he reeled in off the coast of Rhode Island.

"Praying and fishing," said Herbert Hoover, "are the only two Presidential activities in which public and press respect the President's right of privacy." Whenever he could, Hoover sought the solitude of a lake or stream filled with fish.

President Herbert Hoover

Benjamin Harrison was one of our most dignified presidents, but not when he went fishing. According to one of his fishing companions, "When he's on a fishing trip, Ben takes his drink of whiskey in the morning. . . . He chews tobacco from a plug he carries in his hip pocket, spits on his worm for luck and cusses when the fish gets away."

Like fishing, the sport of hunting has been a favorite pastime for several of our presidents. Washington, Benjamin Harrison, Cleveland and Lyndon Johnson were all accomplished hunters. The greatest presidential hunter by far, however, was Theodore Roosevelt. Teddy Roosevelt was a man of many contradictions. On one hand, he was a great conservationist and was responsible for the establishment of our national parks system. On the other hand, he loved hunting big game. Among his trophies was a nine-foot grizzly bear he shot. During an eleven-month African hunting trip he took after leaving the presidency, Roosevelt bagged 296 animals.

While hunting, Teddy Roosevelt once refused to shoot a bear cub. The incident inspired a political cartoon that, in turn, inspired a toy manufacturer to create a new product. It was the Teddy Bear, still popular around the world.

Many of our presidents have loved the game of golf. Woodrow Wilson was probably the most ardent of all presidential golfers. He played every day before breakfast, even in the winter when he used a black ball so he could find it in the snow. Each of our golfing presidents has made his own special impression on the golf course, none more so than William Howard Taft.

Dwight Eisenhower, like Wilson, was passionate about the game of golf. He is our only president to have scored every golfer's dream, a hole in one. While he was in office, cartoonists found his love of the game, his devotion to card playing, and his passion for fishing wonderful subjects for the caricatures they drew of this popular president.

President Taft was so large that he once got stuck in the White House bathtub and had to be rescued. A special bathtub, big enough for four average-sized men, was then built for him.

President John F. Kennedy

The open sea has also been a great attraction for many of our presidents. Several owned their own sailing vessels and spent as much time as they could away from the land and out of the public eye. Franklin Roosevelt and John F. Kennedy were especially attracted to the sea. Before becoming president, Roosevelt had served as assistant secretary of the Navy, while Kennedy had been a naval hero during World War II. Both of these chief executives maintained a "summer White House" along the shore—Roosevelt at Campobello Island in Maine, and Kennedy on Cape Cod.

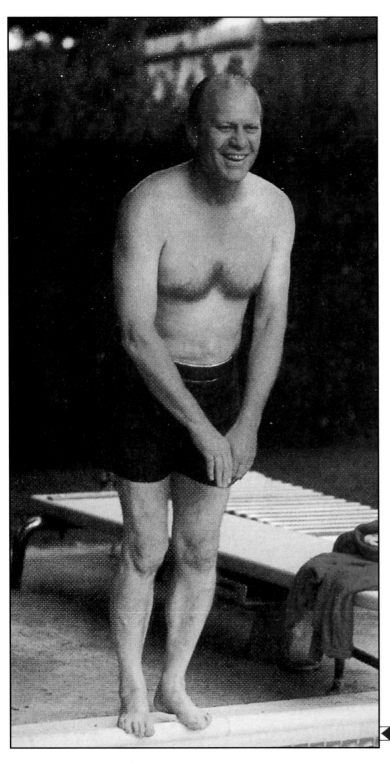

The leisure-time activities of our most recent presidents have reflected the more active lifestyles of modern Americans. While he was chief executive, Gerald Ford kept himself fit by swimming regularly in the White House pool.

Several of our chief executives were accomplished athletes before they became president. Dwight Eisenhower played football for West Point. George Bush played first base for Yale. John Kennedy was a member of the Harvard swimming team, while Jimmy Carter was a cross-country runner at the Naval Academy. Gerald Ford was named the most valuable player on the University of Michigan football team and received professional football offers from the Detroit Lions and the Green Bay Packers.

In the last decades of the twentieth century, Americans have become more health- and exercise-conscious than ever before. Recent presidents have reflected this trend in their off-duty activities. Some of our earlier chief executives were also committed to strenuous exercise. Calvin Coolidge worked out with Indian clubs. Benjamin Harrison used a rowing machine. Herbert Hoover regularly tossed a medicine ball around with members of his cabinet. Several modern presidents have adopted a regular jogging routine, using this form of strenuous exercise to keep fit and to relieve the stress of their responsibilities.

President Jimmy Carter

President Bill Clinton

THE FIRST LADY

Although hobbies and sports have helped many presidents cope with the stress of running the country, our chief executives have received the most comfort and support from their own families. It is not easy being a presidential wife or child. Almost everything they do is under the glare of the public eye. It has been a particular challenge for those women who carry the title "First Lady." Presidents' wives are not elected, are not paid and have no constitutional authority. Yet they are expected to carry out a host of increasingly important duties. Within this broad range of duties, one of the most important has always been that of providing vital support to her husband, the president.

Most of our presidents' wives have also been mothers. Like all mothers, they have experienced the joys and tragedies of parenthood and have raised their children with varying degrees of success. Unlike almost all other mothers, the president's wife is expected to be a role model for the nation while carrying out her motherly responsibilities within the fishbowl that is the White House.

Betty Ford

Edith Roosevelt

The term first lady seems to have originated with a reporter covering the 1877 inauguration of Rutherford Hayes, who referred to his wife, Lucy, as "the First Lady." The term became popular in 1911, when a play about Dolley Madison titled The First Lady in the Land, *became a smash hit.*

There is yet another role that all of our first ladies have been expected to fulfill. Along with being first wife and first mother, the president's wife is expected to be the nation's hostess. It is her responsibility to preside at official White House dinners and other functions and to serve as hostess to visiting dignitaries and other guests. One of the most successful of all White House hostesses was Dolley Madison. She was widely celebrated for the grace and glamour she brought to the role. Some 150 years later, Jacqueline Kennedy earned a similar reputation for her grace and style. From Mary Lincoln entertaining a group of Native Americans to Hillary Rodham Clinton showing visitors through the White House, the role of the president's wife as first hostess has been important to the presidency.

Mary Todd Lincoln

There was a good reason why Dolley Madison was such a successful White House hostess. Unlike any other first lady, she had been given the opportunity to practice the role. Before her husband became president, she had served as the official hostess for Thomas Jefferson, who was a widower.

President Gerald Ford and Betty Ford

Many of our presidents' wives have relished their position as first lady. Others have been less happy in the role. When Margaret Taylor heard of Zachary Taylor's nomination, she said it was "a plot to deprive her of his [company] and shorten his life by unnecessary care and responsibility." Upon hearing the news of Franklin Pierce's nomination, an anguished Jane Pierce promptly fainted. Julia Grant, on the other hand, loved every minute she served as first lady. When Ulysses Grant's time in office was over, she wrote, "My life at the White House was a bright and beautiful dream. . . . I wish it might have continued forever." None of these women would have even considered the possibility of being asked to actively campaign for their husbands' elections or reelections. Yet today our first ladies are now expected to take on still another role—that of political campaigner.

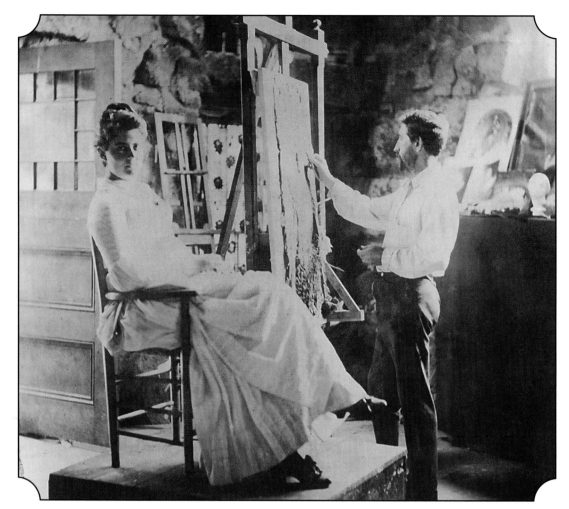

Frances Folsom Cleveland was a highly personable first lady. Her popularity was so great that when her husband ran for president a second time, his campaign managers made the unprecedented move of including her picture on their campaign posters along with those of her husband and his vice presidential running mate.

Like their husbands, our presidents' wives have come from many different backgrounds and in all shapes and sizes. One of the most interesting of all our first ladies was Frances Folsom Cleveland. When she married her husband in the White House at age twenty-one, she became the youngest first lady we have ever had. She was also considered to be one of the most beautiful. Women throughout the nation scanned monthly magazines seeking illustrations of her so that they could copy her latest hairstyle.

As perhaps the most glamorous of all our first ladies, Jacqueline Kennedy set fashion trends for women throughout the world. An accomplished and highly intelligent woman with a deep love of the arts, she made the White House a greater center of culture than it had ever been before. She became famous for the way she acquired furniture, paintings, and other objects, and she renovated the Executive Mansion, making it into a living museum of the presidency.

John Kennedy was well aware of the ways in which his first lady's worldwide popularity and charm contributed to his presidency. At a luncheon on the last day of a successful diplomatic trip to France, he stated, "I do not think it altogether inappropriate to introduce myself. I am the man who accompanied Jacqueline Kennedy to France."

Jacqueline Kennedy Onassis will also be remembered for the extraordinary courage she displayed after the tragedy of her young husband's assassination. Her dignity helped the nation through one of its darkest moments. When she died in May 1994, the nation accorded her a greater display of affection and respect than it had demonstrated for any other first lady.

Just as individual presidents have been instrumental in changing the nature of the presidency, certain first ladies have changed the role and the position of the president's wife as well. Sarah Polk was probably the first first lady to have real political influence upon her husband. She served as his private secretary before James Polk became president, and she continued to do so after they entered the White House. She read through the newspapers for him, briefed him on national and world events and kept him up to date when he was out of Washington. Helen Taft also had a particular influence on the way first ladies were perceived. Aware of the many duties she was expected to carry out in support of her newly elected husband, William Howard Taft, she insisted on sharing in the glory of his victory. On March 4, 1909, Helen Taft proudly became the first president's wife to ride beside him to his inauguration.

Louisa Adams, wife of John Quincy Adams, was the first (and only) foreign-born first lady. Dolley Madison was the first (and only) one to take snuff. Rachel Jackson was the first to smoke pipes and cigars. Priscilla Tyler was the first who had been a professional actress. Lucy Hayes was the first to have graduated from college. Abigail Fillmore was the first to earn her own living before marriage. Florence Harding was the first divorced woman to serve as first lady.

Lou Hoover was one of the first to assume the role of first lady as activist. Like her husband, Herbert Hoover, she was an expert in metallurgy. She spoke four languages fluently and could understand two others. Not content with devoting all her time to either home or social affairs, she became an energetic worker for the League of Women Voters and the General Federation of Women's Clubs. She took on her biggest challenge when she became president of the Girl Scouts of America.

Edith Wilson was probably the most controversial of all our first ladies. When Woodrow Wilson suffered a serious stroke which did leave him paralyzed, though it did not affect his mind, she refused to let him resign. Instead, she took on the role of deciding who should be allowed to meet with him and what matters should be brought to his attention. She was the subject of much criticism from those who, behind her back, called her Mrs. President. Yet, thanks to her, Woodrow Wilson was able to successfully complete the last two years of his second term.

Whenever Lou Hoover and Herbert Hoover did not want to be overheard by White House guests, they spoke to each other in Chinese. Edith Wilson was Woodrow Wilson's second wife. His first wife, Ellen, died during the president's first term in office. During their twenty-nine years of marriage, Woodrow and Ellen Wilson exchanged some 1,400 love letters.

The woman who still serves as the model for the role of first lady as activist was Franklin Roosevelt's wife, Eleanor. In many ways, she was the most remarkable of all our presidents' wives. During her more than twelve years as first lady, she worked closely with members of her husband's administration to create work projects for the unemployed, particularly for women and young people. She created work projects for unemployed professionals such as writers, artists, musicians and actors. She was particularly active in promoting projects designed to better the life of African Americans. Instrumental in the establishment of the National Youth Administration, she insisted that the African-American educator Mary McLeod Bethune be placed on its advisory board to ensure the participation of young African Americans in the program. In addition to these and many other activities, Eleanor Roosevelt was the first first lady to write her own daily newspaper column and to hold formal press conferences. She received more than 250,000 letters a year and answered many of them personally.

Franklin Roosevelt was well aware of his wife's ability to get her own way. "Never get into an argument with the Missus, you can't win," he told a reporter. "You think you have her pinned down here . . . but she bobs up right away over there! No use—you can't win!"

L ike her first cousin Theodore Roosevelt, Eleanor Roosevelt was a person who could not stand still. She was the first first lady to travel by airplane. During her time in the White House, she traveled an average of 40,000 miles a year by plane, train, boat and automobile. Her travels on behalf of her husband's administration took her to almost every part of the globe, where she met with individuals ranging from a Maori tribeswoman to the queen of England. After her husband died, she became the first president's widow to serve the federal government in an executive position when she was appointed by Harry Truman to the United States delegation to the United Nations General Assembly.

Eleanor Roosevelt traveled so far and so often during World War II that the Secret Service assigned her a special code name—Rover. Mrs. Roosevelt insisted on driving her own car and refused Secret Service protection. As a compromise, she agreed to keep a pistol in the glove compartment.

Some of our first ladies, while active in several areas, have become noted for championing a particular cause. For Lyndon Johnson's wife, Lady Bird, that cause was the beautification of America. Thanks to her efforts, in 1965 Congress passed the Highway Beautification Act designed to limit billboards on federal highways and encourage better planning of the nation's roads. Lady Bird gave many speeches emphasizing the close connection between ugliness and crime and initiated the establishment of gardens and parks throughout the nation. She gave special attention to Washington, D.C., where, through her encouragement, the beauty of the national capital was enhanced by countless flowers and trees.

Betty Ford was an accomplished dancer. While she was first lady, her special cause was cultural exchange between American artists and performers and their counterparts in foreign countries. Mrs. Ford's activities were described as having "done more to cement relations . . . than all the talk of diplomats."

"I go upstairs and try to grab a nap in the afternoon," President Lyndon Johnson once told his friends, "but Lady Bird . . . [has] a whole group of people in the next room talking about daffodils."

Along with being activists, several of our more recent first ladies have assumed yet another role, that of political partner to their husbands. It is a role that requires a delicate balance. The American public is wary of first ladies' having too much political influence on their husbands. The evolving role of modern women in the workplace creates a situation in which a first lady's input on a variety of issues can be vital to a president's success. Rosalyn Carter, for example, served as a true political partner to Jimmy Carter. She attended cabinet meetings, toured foreign countries as the president's representative, headed an important commission on mental health, and was an important influence on many of the decisions he made as chief executive.

The popularity of our first ladies has been as varied as that of their husbands. One of the most popular of all our presidents' wives was Barbara Bush, whose quiet dignity endeared her to much of the nation. Mrs. Bush made children's literacy her own special cause and spent many hours reading to young people. When her husband, George Bush, was defeated in his bid for a second term, one of his top campaign managers was heard to state, "We made a big mistake; we should have run Barbara."

Jacqueline Kennedy conducted an "inquiring photographer" column for a Washington newspaper before becoming first lady. Lady Bird Johnson owned and ran a radio station. Betty Ford was a professional model. Pat Nixon was an extra in several Hollywood movies. Nancy Reagan was a full-fledged movie star and appeared opposite her husband, Ronald, in the film Hellcats of the Navy.

The background, style and activities of First Lady Hillary Rodham Clinton serve as an example of the increasingly important public role of women in American life in general and as first lady in particular. An accomplished lawyer who earned far more money in her career than did her husband in his pre–White House days, Hillary Rodham Clinton has been an important part of her husband's administration from the moment of his inauguration. When she was appointed to head a committee to prepare legislation to overhaul the nation's health care system, she assumed the highest official post ever assigned to a first lady. Through her contributions to both the nation and the presidency, she gives real meaning to the statement of one political writer who has observed, "When the American people elect a president, they get two people for the price of one."

PRESIDENTIAL CHILDREN

The White House has always been much more than the place where the president works. It is also his home, and nothing has enlivened the Executive Mansion more than the almost two hundred children and grandchildren who have lived there. The first youngsters to live in the White House were the grandchildren of our second president, John Adams. One of this president's favorite forms of recreation was to pull his little grandson around the Executive Mansion on a kitchen chair. Like those of fathers and grandfathers everywhere, our presidents' lives have been enriched by the children who have surrounded them.

Several of our presidents have been particularly close to their children. As the nation's commander in chief during the Civil War, Abraham Lincoln had few pleasurable moments. Most of these were spent in the company of his sons, Tad, Willie and Robert. Though one of our greatest presidents, Lincoln was a man destined for tragedy. As if presiding over a nation which had split itself apart was not sad enough, his life was made even more tragic when twelve-year-old Willie contracted typhoid fever and died in the White House.

Like Abraham Lincoln, President James Garfield was a man marked for tragedy. He was the father of seven children but lost two of them to disease. Like Lincoln, he was also assassinated while in office. During the seven months he lived in the White House, he was particularly close to his only daughter, Molly, to whom he read whenever he could steal away from his official duties.

Abraham Lincoln, John Adams, Thomas Jefferson, Calvin Coolidge and John Kennedy all suffered the loss of a child while serving as president. Franklin Pierce's son died between the time Pierce was elected and inaugurated.

PRESIDENT TYLER'S PARTY FOR CHILDREN.

The first child born to a president and his wife in the White House was Esther Cleveland. She was the subject of great media attention, and the White House was flooded with baby gifts from around the country. Esther had a sister, Ruth, who was born two years before her when their parents were out of the White House between President Cleveland's two nonconsecutive terms. Baby Ruth was also extremely popular, so much so that she even had a candy bar named for her.

The first girl born in the White House was John Tyler's granddaughter, Letitia. Little Letitia entered an already crowded family, for John Tyler had fifteen children of his own, more than any other chief executive. Tyler's youngest child was born when he was seventy years old. During his days in the White House, this president was fond of giving parties for his children and grandchildren and for their young friends. These parties were always crowded and lively affairs.

No president of the United States was an only child.

The tradition of a National Easter Egg Roll actually began on the grounds of the United States Capitol Building. When various congressmen complained that the activities were ruining the national grass, Lucy Hayes, who loved children, had the event moved to the White House lawn, where it has been held ever since.

Throughout the years, the White House has played host not only to the children and grandchildren of our presidents, but to countless other youngsters as well. In the nineteenth century, for example, children from Washington and surrounding areas were invited to May Day activities that included dances held around a giant May Pole on the White House lawn. A children's event that still is on the White House calendar is the annual Easter Egg Roll. At this event, tens of thousands of children are admitted to the south lawn of the Executive Mansion, where they compete in egg-rolling contests, hunt for Easter eggs and are entertained by magicians, storytellers and clowns.

In many ways, being a president's child is not an easy experience. The need for security and the glare of the public eye make a normal childhood difficult to maintain. Margaret Truman referred to the White House as "the Great White Jail" and refused to become engaged while living there because she felt she could never be sure whether her suitors liked her for herself or because she was the president's daughter. Still, many presidential children have led almost normal lives while in the White House. The most boisterous youngsters ever to inhabit the Executive Mansion were Theodore Roosevelt's children who inherited their father's love of mischief. Young Quentin Roosevelt organized his classmates into the White House Gang that, among other pranks, dropped a giant snowball off a White House balcony onto a policeman. Quentin's sister Ethel loved to "toboggan" down the White House stairs on a cookie sheet. Their sister Alice was the greatest mischief-maker of all. Asked why he couldn't make Alice behave, Teddy Roosevelt replied, "I can run the country or control Alice, but not both."

Quentin and Kermit Roosevelt

Three of Theodore Roosevelt's four sons died while in military service. Quentin was shot down in aerial combat over France in 1918; Kermit died on active duty in Alaska in 1943; and Theodore, Jr., died of a heart attack in France in 1944 after becoming a military hero.

President Theodore Roosevelt
and Theodore Roosevelt, Jr.

Despite the challenges of life in the White House, many presidential children have gone on to achieve rich and successful lives. Herbert Hoover, Jr., for example, became an important inventor who received patents for his oil-locating devices. Robert Taft had a distinguished career in the United States Senate, while two of Franklin Roosevelt's sons served in the U.S. House of Representatives. Five presidents' sons received the nomination of their party for president, while three sons of presidents served in other presidents' cabinets. Both Theodore Roosevelt, Jr., who was an excellent horseman like his father, and Rutherford Hayes's son, Webb, became military heroes and were awarded the Congressional Medal of Honor.

Lynda Bird Johnson and Charles Robb

In 1820, Maria Monroe became the first president's child to be married in the White House. The other presidents' children to be wed in the Executive Mansion were: Elizabeth Tyler, Nellie Grant, Alice Roosevelt, Jessie Wilson, Eleanor Wilson, Lynda Bird Johnson and Tricia Nixon.

In modern times, the glare of publicity has fallen almost as heavily on their children as on our presidents and their wives. The public, it seems, has an insatiable appetite for news about presidential sons and daughters. This is particularly true when a first family wedding is involved. White House weddings such as that of Lynda Bird Johnson to Charles Robb, and Tricia Nixon to Edward Cox, take on the flavor of royal affairs.

Despite all the attention that is heaped upon them, most presidential children have worked hard at leading as normal a life as possible. Amy Carter spent many happy hours playing with her friends in a tree house on the White House grounds.

Susan Ford was a teenager when her father served as president. Rather than let her White House address interfere with her teenage activities, she took advantage of it. She even persuaded her parents to allow her classmates to hold the first high-school senior prom ever at the Executive Mansion. Here she is pictured third from the right.

Susan Ford worked in the White House before her father did. During the Nixon presidency, she sold guidebooks to tourists.

Along with the drawbacks, there are, of course, many advantages to being a president's child. The White House can be one of the most exciting places in the world, filled with historic events and exciting people. Memories are established that will last a lifetime. Can anyone doubt that Chelsea Clinton will always remember standing next to her father as he was sworn in as president of the United States, or that she will ever forget attending one of the inaugural balls that followed his swearing-in?

The children of our presidents have brought laughter and joy to the White House and have added a needed human touch as only children can. They have contributed real services as well. Through the years, many have served as representatives of the president or the first lady, particularly at events involving young people. When Julie Nixon conducted her White House tours, she was not only giving visiting youngsters an appreciation of an important part of their history; she was personally demonstrating the importance of every member of the first family to the presidential experience.

Before he became president, Richard Nixon served as vice president to Dwight Eisenhower. On her various trips to the White House, Julie Nixon got to know one of Eisenhower's grandchildren, David. They fell in love and later married, further uniting two presidential families.

PRESIDENTIAL PETS

While they are special in many ways, our first families, like families everywhere, have had their lives enriched by their pets. Over the years, the Executive Mansion has been home to almost every type of pet imaginable. There have been scores of common pets such as horses, dogs, cats and birds, but there have been many unusual animals as well. Teddy Roosevelt's children had a one-legged rooster. President Hoover's son Alan had two pet alligators that sometimes wandered loose around the White House. Many of our first families have kept nothing less than a menagerie of pets. The Kennedys, for example, had several dogs, a cat, a horse, three ponies, a hamster and a rabbit.

When William Henry Harrison was president, he gave his grandchildren a goat. When one of his grandchildren, Benjamin, became president, he carried on the tradition. Benjamin Harrison gave his own grandchildren a goat to play with on the White House grounds.

GENERAL ZACHARIAH TAYLOR, (OLD ROUGH AND READY.)
As he appeared at the battle of Palo Alto; from a sketch by a lieutenant of Artillery.

From the first days of the first presidency, horses have ranked among the most favorite of all first family pets. Zachary Taylor, like several other early chief executives who had been military leaders, owed much to the horses that had served him so well on the battlefield. When he moved into the Executive Mansion, he brought his favorite mount, Whitey, with him and tethered the animal on the White House lawn. The horse soon had to be moved inside a White House stable, though, when visitors, anxious to obtain any kind of presidential souvenir, began to pluck hairs from poor Whitey's tail.

President Franklin Pierce also liked to race his horse and carriage through the streets of Washington. On one of his jaunts he was arrested for running down an elderly woman. The charges against him could not be proven, and the case was dismissed.

As a military leader in both the Mexican and Civil wars, Ulysses S. Grant had spent much of his life on horseback. When he became president, his horses and ponies filled the White House stables. Grant loved to race through the streets of Washington in an open horse-drawn carriage. On one occasion, he was stopped and fined by a policeman who didn't recognize him as the president of the United States.

Horses and ponies have been pets of presidents' children as well. Young Caroline Kennedy spent many happy childhood hours on the back of her favorite pet, Macaroni. Caroline and her pony received much attention from the White House press corps and from the public. In fact, Macaroni received thousands of letters from young fans across the nation.

Our presidents have always understood the appeal that presidential pets have for the American public. After many lessons, a dog handler taught Caroline Kennedy's dog, Pushinka, to climb the steps up to Caroline's tree house. On the day he made his first successful climb, photographers were present to record it. As the cameras clicked, a smiling President Kennedy stated, "That's worth six million votes right there."

Dogs have been the most popular White House pet by far. One of the most celebrated and pampered of all White House dogs was Warren Harding's Airedale, Laddie Boy. Every day, Laddie Boy, who owned Washington Dog License Number 1, delivered the president's newspapers to him. Laddie Boy had his own White House valet and once had a birthday party at which a frosted cake made of many layers of dog biscuits was served. When President Harding died while in office, the Newsboys' Association asked every newsboy in America to donate a penny toward a statue of Laddie Boy to be erected in the president's honor. The statue now stands in the Smithsonian Institution.

Warren Harding once used the president's power to grant clemency to save the life of a dog. The animal had been brought into the United States illegally, and a Pennsylvania judge ordered it put to death. Harding made a personal plea to the governor of Pennsylvania, who officially pardoned the dog.

Gerald Ford's golden retriever, Liberty, was a close companion to the president. While Ford was in the White House, Liberty performed an important service for his owner. When a visitor stayed too long in the Oval Office, Ford would signal the dog to rush into the office, creating a disruption that would allow the president to end the meeting.

Like Harding's Laddie Boy, Franklin D. Roosevelt's Scottie, Fala, became a huge favorite of the American public. The much-traveled president took the dog almost everywhere he journeyed. On one official trip aboard the USS *Baltimore*, Fala suffered a fate similar to that of Zachary Taylor's horse, Whitey. Sailors aboard the vessel, anxious to obtain presidential souvenirs, cut so many hairs from the dog that the animal was left almost totally bald. The furious president, while continuing to make the dog his traveling companion, made sure that never happened again.

Each of our first families has received many gifts sent by admirers from the United States and around the world. Many of these gifts have been animals that the senders have hoped the first families would adopt. First family members have to be careful about publicly stating their love of a particular animal, as Woodrow Wilson found out when he expressed his fondness for birds.

Thomas Jefferson kept a mockingbird in his White House study. The pet often rode on Jefferson's shoulder and was trained by the president to take food from his lips.

Some of the animals that have lived at the White House have come there as a result of historical events. During World War I, President Wilson and his family released the White House groundskeepers so they could help the war effort. In order to keep the grass trimmed around the Executive Mansion, the Wilsons kept a flock of sheep on the White House lawn. One of the sheep was Old Ike, a ram that loved to chew tobacco.

The family of William Howard Taft had its own unusual pet. Her name was Pauline, and she was a cow. While the Tafts served as the first family, Pauline grazed freely on both the White House lawns and the grounds of the Executive Office Building next door.

The list of White House pets includes nearly everything that can walk, swim, crawl or fly. Badgers, lizards, snakes, turtles, turkeys, hyenas and coyotes have all been part of the collective White House menagerie. Grace Coolidge had her own very special pet, a raccoon that had been sent to the Coolidges to be cooked as an exotic Thanksgiving Day dinner treat. Mrs. Coolidge was appalled at the idea and adopted the animal as a playful companion.

Calvin and Grace Coolidge and their children had one of the largest collections of pets of any of our first families. Over the years their pets included a goose, a wallaby, a donkey, a thrush, a lion cub, two cats, twelve dogs and several birds.

White House pets have made an important contribution toward easing the burdens of every first family. Most important, they have helped remind us that, despite the power and grandeur that goes with it, the presidency is, after all, a very human institution.

President Lyndon Johnson

THE HIGHEST OFFICE IN THE LAND

The American presidency is filled with symbols and slogans. Far more importantly, it is dominated by the people who have accepted enormous challenges and have done their best to meet them.

President Jimmy Carter and Martin Luther King, Sr.

We owe much to these leaders who, despite personal and national disappointments and tragedies, have made the well-being of the United States their personal responsibility.

"May none but honest and wise men rule under this roof."
—Carving on a White House mantelpiece

W e also owe an enormous debt to our presidents' families. They have performed a vital service to the men they call husband or father or grandfather or son. In countless ways, they have contributed significantly both to the life of the presidency and to the nation.

President Franklin D. Roosevelt and family

PRESIDENTS OF THE UNITED STATES

1. George Washington
Born February 22, 1732
Died December 14, 1799
Term: 1789–1797

2. John Adams
Born October 30, 1735
Died July 4, 1826
Term: 1797–1801

3. Thomas Jefferson
Born April 13, 1743
Died July 4, 1826
Term: 1801–1809

4. James Madison
Born March 16, 1751
Died June 28, 1836
Term: 1809–1817

5. James Monroe
Born April 28, 1758
Died July 4, 1831
Term: 1817–1825

6. John Quincy Adams
Born July 11, 1767
Died February 23, 1848
Term: 1825–1829

7. Andrew Jackson
Born March 15, 1767
Died June 8, 1845
Term: 1829–1837

8. Martin Van Buren
Born December 5, 1782
Died July 24, 1862
Term: 1837–1841

9. William Henry Harrison
Born February 9, 1773
Died April 4, 1841
Term: 1841

10. John Tyler
Born Mach 29, 1790
Died January 18, 1862
Term: 1841–1845

11. James Knox Polk
Born November 2, 1795
Died June 15, 1849
Term: 1845–1849

12. Zachary Taylor
Born November 24, 1784
Died July 8, 1850
Term: 1849–1850

13. Millard Fillmore
Born January 7, 1800
Died March 8, 1874
Term: 1850–1853

14. Franklin Pierce
Born November 23, 1804
Died October 8, 1869
Term: 1853–1857

15. James Buchanan
Born April 23, 1791
Died June 1, 1868
Term: 1857–1861

16. Abraham Lincoln
Born February 12, 1809
Died April 15, 1865
Term: 1861–1865

17. Andrew Johnson
Born December 29, 1808
Died July 31, 1875
Term: 1865–1869

18. Ulysses Simpson Grant
Born April 27, 1822
Died July 23, 1885
Term: 1869–1877

19. Rutherford Birchard Hayes
Born October 4, 1822
Died January 17, 1893
Term: 1877–1881

20. James Abram Garfield
Born November 19, 1831
Died September 19, 1881
Term: 1881

21. Chester Alan Arthur
Born October 5, 1830
Died November 18, 1886
Term: 1881–1885

22. Stephen Grover Cleveland
Born March 18, 1837
Died June 24, 1908
Term: 1885–1889

23. Benjamin Harrison
Born August 20, 1833
Died March 13, 1901
Term: 1889–1893

24. Stephen Grover Cleveland
Term: 1893–1897

25. William McKinley
Born January 29, 1843
Died September 14, 1901
Term: 1897–1901

26. Theodore Roosevelt
Born October 27, 1858
Died January 6, 1919
Term: 1901–1909

27. William Howard Taft
Born September 15, 1857
Died March 8, 1930
Term: 1909–1913

28. Thomas Woodrow Wilson
Born December 29, 1856
Died February 3, 1924
Term: 1913–1921

29. Warren Gamaliel Harding
Born November 2, 1865
Died August 2, 1923
Term: 1921–1923

30. John Calvin Coolidge
Born July 4, 1872
Died January 5, 1933
Term: 1923–1929

31. Herbert Clark Hoover
Born August 10, 1874
Died October 20, 1964
Term: 1929–1933

32. Franklin Delano Roosevelt
Born January 30, 1882
Died April 12, 1945
Term: 1933–1945

33. Harry S. Truman
Born May 8, 1884
Died December 26, 1972
Term: 1945–1953

34. Dwight David Eisenhower
Born October 14, 1890
Died March 28, 1969
Term: 1953–1961

35. John Fitzgerald Kennedy
Born May 29, 1917
Died November 22, 1963
Term: 1961–1963

36. Lyndon Baines Johnson
Born August 27, 1908
Died January 22, 1973
Term: 1963–1969

37. Richard Milhous Nixon
Born January 9, 1913
Died April 22, 1994
Term: 1969–1974

38. Gerald Rudolf Ford
Born July 14, 1913
Term: 1974–1977

39. James Earl Carter
Born October 1, 1924
Term: 1977–1981

40. Ronald Wilson Reagan
Born February 6, 1911
Term: 1981–1989

41. George Herbert Walker Bush
Born June 12, 1924
Term: 1989–1993

42. William Jefferson Clinton
Born August 19, 1946
Term: 1992–

The Library of Congress

Most of the photographs, lithographs, engravings, paintings, line drawings, posters, broadsides and other illustrative materials contained in this book have been culled from the collections of the Library of Congress. The Library houses the largest collection of stored knowledge in the world. Within its walls lie treasures that show us how much more than a "library" a great library can be.

The statistics that help define the Library are truly amazing. It has more books from America and England than anywhere else, yet barely one half of its collections are in English. It contains more maps, globes, charts and atlases than any other place on earth. It houses one of the largest collections of photographs in the world, the largest collection of films in America, almost every phonograph record ever made in the United States and the collections of the American Folklife Center. The Library also contains over six million volumes on hard sciences and technology.

It's a very modern institution as well. Dr. James Billington, the Librarian of Congress, has defined the Library's future through his vision of a "library without walls." "I see the Library of Congress in the future," he has said, "as an active catalyst for civilization, not just a passive mausoleum of cultural accomplishments of the past."

The Library of Congress was originally established to serve the members of Congress. Over the years it has evolved into a great national library. Unlike almost every other national library in the world, the Library of Congress does not limit the use of its collections to accredited scholars. Ours is a national library made by the people for the people, and is open to all the people. Fondly referred to as "the storehouse of our national memory," it is truly one of our proudest and most important possessions.

Index

Numbers in *italics* indicate photographs and illustrations.

White House
    carving on mantelpiece in, 83
    children born in, 64, *64*
    first children in, 62
    host to children of public, 65, *65*
    improvements made in, 21
    inaugural party for Andrew Jackson, 33, *33*
    public receptions, 37
    renovations by Kennedy, Jacqueline, 53
    romance begun in, 71
    weddings in, *26*, 68, *68*
White House Gang, 66
Whitey, 74, *74*
Wilson, Edith, 55, *55*
Wilson, Eleanor, 68
Wilson, Ellen, 55
Wilson, Henry, *9*
Wilson, Jessie, 68
Wilson, Woodrow, 29, 44, 55, *55*, 78, *78*, 79
women
    first cabinet member, 22
    first presidential candidate, 19
    public role of, 61
    See also first ladies
Woodhull, Victoria Claflin, 19
World War II, 22

Youngest president, 13